Introduction
by Ken Coates

On 8-9 May 2004 meets the founding congress of the Party of the European Left. This brings together a number of the left parties in Europe, including several which are constituent members of the European United Left-Nordic Green Left, a recognised political grouping within the European Parliament.

These documents propose 'a broad social and political alliance' to promote significant changes of policy in the societies which comprise the enlarged European Union. The need for closer co-operation between the separate forces of the European Left is increasingly obvious: the depredations of neo-liberalism, and the growth of a warlike culture which is already dividing the governments of Europe, and provoking huge protests from their peoples, underline this necessity every day.

For further information about the European Left, please contact the Initiative Group, care of 00161 Roma, Viale del Policlinico, 131, Italy.

* * *

Manifesto of the European Left
Joint draft of the initiative-group to establish the
Party of the European Left (EL), Berlin 10-11 January 2004

New hope is springing up in Europe. A new vision is inspiring more and more Europeans and uniting them in great mobilisations to resist the imposition of a capitalist one-way street, which is an attempt to trap humanity in a new social and cultural regression. The conditions prevailing for peoples, social organisations and individuals are marked by insecurity, uncertainty and hazards. New resistance to capitalist exploitation is being expressed strongly. A new option for change has touched the lives of men and women who are increasingly affected by the disasters brought about by capitalist globalisation policies.

The new forms of power on a worldwide scale have precipitated crises in nation states, in alliance systems and in the post-World War Two global order. The theory of permanent war, as currently put forward by the Bush doctrine, and the vortex of terrorist violence that war nourishes, cause inequalities to increase and democracy to be diminished.

Europe is for us a place for the regeneration of struggle for a better society. The scope of this undertaking will include the achievement of peace and the transformation of today's capitalist society. We strive for a society that transcends capitalist and patriarchal logic. Our aim is human emancipation, the liberation of women and men from all forms of oppression, exploitation and exclusion.

We perceive the role and the task of the European Left as contributing to the formation of a broad social and political alliance to promote radical changes of policy by developing concrete alternatives and proposals to transform the present capitalist societies. We see in it our responsibility to address all those taking action for a more equitable society as a condition for their own self-determined life. We want to establish the politics of the Left as a permanent, independent, confident political voice that will contribute to implementing solidarity and democratic, social and ecological alternatives.

For this reason the European Union, and indeed the European continent as a whole – in addition to the traditional political levels of nation-states, regions and municipalities – is becoming an increasingly important place for alternative politics and interwoven with world developments.

Therefore we see the universal scope of the anti-globalist movement, its growing exchanges, mutual co-operation and influence on traditional social, labour, feminist, environmentalist and democratic movements as fresh participation in the fight for change. All these movements propose – in opposition to the 'private space' of the major world powers – a 'public space' inhabited by citizens who want to reclaim fundamental rights such as peace, democracy, social justice, freedom, gender equality and respect for nature. These movements include the political Left.

In many European countries, profound cultural and political experiences and social struggles marked the original character of the

European social model. We look to these political and cultural roots, rather than to the market values that define it today, especially the Maastricht treaty policies and the decisions of the European Central Bank.

In each of our European countries, people are suffering from the policies of globalised capitalism implemented by governments in the interest of big capital and lobbies. These policies undermine the solidarity and social gains won through struggle. There is a general attack on pension systems; social security systems are being dismantled and privatised; public services and essential sectors such as health, education, culture and utilities including water and other natural resources are being subjugated to the law of the market; the labour market is being deregulated and more and more jobs are becoming part-time. Anti-trade union repression is being stepped up and migration criminalised.

Everything has become a commodity, from labour through the whole life cycle. In Europe today there is growing unemployment, insecurity, external militarisation as demonstrated in Bosnia and Kosovo, Afghanistan and Iraq, and internal militarisation through repressive laws against those who oppose neo-liberal policies. This process is alienating ever larger numbers of people from politics; it is causing wars between the poor; and it is responsible for the resurgence of populism, racism and fanaticism.

The social democratic Third Way failed in Europe because it was unable to resist this trend and, having no alternative, actually promoted it. This failure creates opportunities but also places a greater responsibility on the Left, which wants to change the world. We must, however, avoid the path taken in the 20th century, which brought great achievements as well as great defeats and tragedies to the forces with revolutionary ideals.

To change society we need to broaden our action. **In Europe the challenge is to build an alternative, radical, environmentalist and feminist Left. The pluralist nature of movements is intersected by this new political force, because we want to build a new relationship between society and politics.**

We want to build another Europe and give a different meaning to the European Union. We want it to be independent of US hegemony, open to the South, a social and political model that provides an alternative to capitalism, strongly opposed to militarisation and war, in favour of environmental protection and respect for human rights, including social and economic ones, and in favour of the right to citizenship for all those living in Europe.

We want a Europe free from the anti-democratic and neo-liberal policies of the World Trade Organisation and the International Monetary Fund, free from NATO, foreign military bases and any model of a European army leading to increasing military conflicts and to a spiralling arms race. We want a Europe of peace and solidarity, free from nuclear weapons and weapons of mass destruction, a Europe that rejects war as an instrument for settling international conflicts. This concerns the Israeli-Palestinian conflict in particular, which should be resolved in accordance with UN resolutions.

We, the parties and political organisations inspired by communist, socialist, democratic, environmentalist, and feminist ideals, who are against neo-liberalism and in favour of social change, want to establish a new political organisation: the Party of the European Left (EL).

It is our hope that we will be able to tackle in fresh terms issues such as globalisation, world peace, democracy, social justice, and gender equality; that we will be able to ensure a self-determined life for handicapped people, sustainable and balanced development, and respect for individual cultural, religious, ideological or sexual choices.

We can see the need for deep-rooted social and democratic change in Europe. We believe the time has come to step up our struggle to challenge the sacrosanct doctrine of the 'free market economy' and the power of financial markets and multinational corporations, and, instead, to make our citizens active agents of the policies implemented in their name.

Faced with the recession and rising unemployment, we must challenge the 'stability pact' and the European Central Bank orientations, and we must work to promote different economic and social policies and priorities that foster environment-friendly full employment and training, public services and a bold investment policy. Capital movement must be taxed, and priorities must be changed in favour of human beings, not money.

We express our commitment to work throughout Europe to

advance the rights of wage-earners in their workplaces. We consider that public services are an indispensable means of guaranteeing everyone's equal rights to education, water, food, health, power and transportation. We are in favour of modernised, decentralised and democratised public services that guarantee equal social rights for all.

Today, ten new countries are joining the European Union, and others have expressed the desire to do likewise. But there are significant political and social forces within these countries and in the countries that are already European Union members, who view enlargement with reservations or outright hostility. The impasses created by the European Union's present strategic choices reinforce these tendencies.

The Party of the European Left also responds to the challenges for countries that are now outside the European Union, such as the Balkan states and other Eastern European countries. These are caused mainly by their transformation, and by the growing dilemma of choosing between independent development and joining capitalist Europe as a middle-term strategy for dealing with the conflicts in these countries related to past and present changes. The European Left is ready to stand by all democratic forces in these countries in support of democracy, peace and social justice, social and economic development, and stronger democratic institutions.

We want to ensure that elected bodies – the European Parliament, national parliaments, and representative committees (such as the Economic and Social Committee and the Committee of the Regions) – have more powers of action and control. Today, whatever may be our overall opinion of the 'Constitutional Treaty' being discussed, we are opposed to a Directorate of Great Powers. We do not accept the effort to impose ultra-liberal economic criteria or militarisation on us, as these will lead to substantial social setbacks.

We will strive unceasingly to broaden the citizens' action, participation and control at all levels and at every stage in the building of Europe.

What is finally at the heart of the crisis in the European Union is democracy. For decades the European Union has been built from above, with disregard for its great diversity of cultures and languages — without its people and often against them

European Left

But something is already beginning to change. The great social, trade union, working class and civic struggles against the war have begun to change the situation. In just a few years these struggles have contributed to rallying broad support for peace, equal rights, and respect for the planet. As political forces for social transformation, we want to contribute to this new dynamic that is resolutely attacking neo-liberal policies. Social forums have provided essential moments of debate, of confrontation and of building popular and political alternatives to today's neo-liberal Europe. Social movements and citizens' struggles have their own dynamics, independent analyses, proposals and initiatives. We are in favour not only of defending the rights of workers and trade unions against all discrimination, but also of extending workers' rights, including benefits for the unemployed and for workers in insecure jobs, extending democracy in the workplace and in economic life, at all levels, including the Europe-wide one.

We stand for social, ecological, and sustainable development and for the restructuring of the economy based on protection of the environment and climate, and on the precautionary principle, through the use of environmentally-friendly technologies, through lifelong social solidarity, through the creation of new jobs and support for the disadvantaged regions of the earth.

We will promote an enhanced role in European decision-making for the Committee of the Regions and the Social and Economic Committee, as substantial statutory organs of democratic and regional policy in the European Union.

In the European Union there are a number of conflicting interests. For us, this creates a new political arena for the class struggle and for defending the interests of workers and democracy, as well as those of European society with its organisations and institutions, including the European Parliament.

The European Left is committed to the fight to make the great changes it espouses become reality – within the context of the constant broadening of peace, democracy and social justice.

Let us fight together for a new society, a world of justice free from exploitation and war. Together we proclaim that another Europe is possible. The future is here; history never ends.

Together for a Different Europe –
Democratic, Social, Ecological, Feminist, Peaceful
The Berlin Appeal for the founding of the European Left Party,
11 January 2004

In Europe and in the world, there is growing resistance to wars, to the destruction of the welfare systems, to the arms build-up, and to market radicalism. We of the European left are part of the movements for a different policy. We are convinced that another world, another Europe, is possible: democratic, social, ecological, feminist, peaceful – a Europe of solidarity.

The time is ripe for a European Left Party. We want to found it before the 2004 European elections take place.

The Other Europe

- After the end of the Cold War, hot war returned. The European Union is being militarised alongside NATO. In Europe there are strong forces aspiring to take their share in the imperial repartition of the world. The United States is trying to integrate Europe into its plans for world domination. That is not our path. We want a Europe free of weapons of mass destruction from the Atlantic to the Urals; a Europe of collective security without NATO and without the European Union as a military alliance; a Europe distinguishing itself with initiatives for disarmament, development, partnership and the reinforcement of international law.
- The gap between rich and poor is deepening on our continent. Millions of people are jobless or in precarious employment. Social security is being destroyed, welfare services privatised. That is not our path. We want solidarity, social rights and a redistribution of social wealth from top to bottom of society, from the rich to the poor. Faced with recession and the growth of unemployment, the 'stability pact' and the European Central Bank orientations must be challenged so as to work towards another economic and social policy, and social priorities in favour of full employment and training, public services and a bold investment policy, for the environment. The taxation of capital flows must be imposed.

The European Left Party

The European Left Party wants to be not only an outward but also an inward alternative to the dominant policy in Europe. Together we want to act transparently, democratically and on terms of equality. Together we want to be more convincing and politically more assertive. We know that we can only acquire that wealth if we preserve and renew our own social and historical experiences, perceptions, traditions and cultures and pool them in common.

Respecting the full independence, sovereignty and individual responsibility of all participating partners, our relationship and cooperation are marked by openness, respect, acceptance and tolerance. At the centre of our thought and action is not profit or power, but the human being. Europe is our common field of action.

We want to put into question profit dominance and overcome the power of capitalism. We want a different culture of living, working, producing and distributing. Our points of reference are the struggle for peace, anti-fascism, anti-racism, democracy, social justice, feminism, and ecology.

We are starting now, and we extend an invitation to take this first step together. We shall remain open to those who do not decide yet or decide otherwise. We have profound esteem for manifold forms of cooperation. We shall practise them, to make our continent a democratic, social, sustainable and peaceful one.

Party of Democratic Socialism (PDS – Germany)
Communist Refoundation Party (Italy)
United Left (Spain)
French Communist Party
Slovakian Communist Party
Communist Party of Bohemia and Moravia (Czech Republic)
Party of Democratic Socialism (Czech Republic)
The Left (Luxemburg)
Coalition of the Left, Movements and Ecology (SYNASPISMOS – Greece)
Estonian Social Democratic Labour Party
Austrian Communist Party

Priorities must be changed – in favour of human beings, not money.
- In the European Union, the Council of Ministers and the Commission have a great deal of power. They make their decisions behind close doors, influenced by lobbyists and private interests. Ordinary men and women have less of a say. The political system is drifting towards a crisis of authority. That is not our path. We want transparency, new forms of democracy and a share in shaping events with ordinary men and women, more power to the national parliaments and to the European Parliament.
- Europe is becoming a fortress. In the name of the 'struggle against terrorism', human and civil rights are restricted and threatened. That is not our path. We want a Europe open to the world, a Europe with strong human and civil rights, where the persecuted are granted asylum.
- Europe is striving for economic dominance. It is waging trade wars. Its monetary, financial and trade policies have a particularly negative effect on the threshold and developing countries. That is not our path. Mindful of the bloody history of colonisation, we want to undertake bold initiatives to develop an equitable economic and political co-operation.
- The diversity of its cultures and ways of life makes Europe a vigorous continent. However, they are in danger of being flattened out. The concentration of the mass media in the hands of a few endangers the plurality of opinions. Information, culture and education are being turned into commodities. That is not our path. We want cultural diversity, education, knowledge, and information for all men and women.
- Europe is one of the main perpetrators of global environmental problems — with its high carbon dioxide emissions, exporting of waste, world-wide exploitation of energy reserves and forests. That is not our path. We want to live and work as ecologically responsible people.
- Progress has been made in the last decades in terms of gender equality and non-discrimination. Nowadays they are especially jeopardised by the neo-liberal policy of deregulation of labour markets. That is not our path. We want to overcome discrimination, we want real and lasting gender democracy.

Published in May 2004 by Spokesman Books for Socialist Renewal,
Russell House, Bulwell Lane, Nottingham, NG6 0BT
phone 0115 970 8318 fax 0115 942 0433
e-mail elfeuro@compuserve.com   www.spokesmanbooks.com

ISBN 0851246907